Reflections in a China Teacup

Simple Thoughts to Living a Serene Life
by Janet Burke

Dedicated to
my Children
and
Grandchildren

"I wanted a perfect ending. Now I've learned the hard way that some poems don't rhyme, and some stories don't have a clear beginning, middle and end. Life is about not knowing, having to change, taking the moment and making the best of it, without knowing what's going to happen next."
- Gilda Radner

Introduction

I am not an expert on anything. I am, however, knowledgeable about SOME things. I happily and thankfully celebrated a milestone birthday this year - my 60th - and believe that our life experiences make us knowledgeable. I've had my share of missteps over the decades, but those perceived failures have been the foundation for growth. I'm still growing and look forward to the decades yet to live.

I have never traveled much, but last year I had the "trip of a lifetime" to Italy. This was not a "tour group" trip. It was a trip that was planned to immerse ourselves in the Italian culture and truly "experience" Italy. Since I had never been overseas before, planning this trip consumed most of my time over the course of a year.

Staying in small family-run hotels and bed-and-breakfast inns provided us the opportunity to meet some very interesting people and experience local customs and foods. There were days that were spent just sitting outside on a patio or in a park marveling at the beauty of a different culture.

My favorite memories of the trip were the wonderful breakfasts. I realize that breakfast is a "grab and go" event in most U. S. households. Breakfast , however, is an "event" in Europe. Every morning we were served a typical Italian breakfast - cheeses, meats, pastries, breads and wonderful coffee and tea. The thing that made the meal so wonderful was in the presentation. The tables in the breakfast rooms were covered in linen tablecloths and the food was served on fine china. The coffee was always brought out in beautiful china teacups. All of the guests would visit with each other during breakfast which provided an opportunity to meet people from all over the world. Those breakfasts were something I looked forward to each morning and gave me a sense of calm and relaxation to start the day.

When I returned home, I noticed the collection of my mother-in-law's china teacups that were "on display." I also noticed my mother's china which was proudly displayed in the china cabinet. I took out the teacups and marveled at their beauty as I dusted them off. I thought to myself that china is to be USED, not displayed. If it gets chipped or broken, it's okay.

I now use the "good" china every day. Drinking my coffee each morning in a china teacup is a treat and gives me time to relax and reflect. Writing down my thoughts each morning while having breakfast on the "good" china brings me much joy. I hope that these reflections will give you a sense of serenity as you move forward in your life.

Write It Down

There is nothing quite as powerful as the written word. How do you feel when you read a hand-written note of concern or love? It most likely gives you a sense of comfort. The nice thing about it is that you can pull out that note whenever you need a "pick-me-up."

Writing can also reinforce an idea or thoughts. For example, when you write down goals for yourself, you are committing those thoughts to paper. You can use it as a check-list and mark off the goals as you complete them which, in turn, will give you a sense of accomplishment. In the same way, you can write down a daily "to-do" list and mark off the things you accomplish throughout the day. This will also help keep you organized.

Writing is also a good way to enhance your overall well-being. Using a journal to write down your feelings is a way to "vent" to yourself about frustration with work or situations in your personal life. Keeping a journal, therefore, gives you an outlet to express your feelings and helps you "think" before you "speak." This, in turn, cuts down on the time you waste on resentment and worry. It is also a way to reflect on all the joys and blessings you have in your life.

Action Step: Write down daily goals.

Smile...and the world smiles

Did you know that your personality shows up through your facial expressions? It's true. When I am on the phone, I can tell whether someone is smiling or frowning just from their tone of voice. A person with a smile on their face has a lighter, kinder sound to their voice. A person with a frown has a deeper, monotone sound. Think about that when you are dealing with family, friends, and co-workers.

Putting a smile on your face as you are walking out the door each day should become a new habit. It immediately puts you in a positive frame of mind and ready to meet the day head-on. It is the least expensive thing that you can put on, but it will impress people much more than a high-dollar suit, expensive manicure, or perfectly coiffed hair.

When dealing with difficult people or situations, a smile can help ease the tension. When you smile, your body naturally relaxes and the tension you might have felt from the encounter is diminished.

A smile makes you more approachable and people will view you as a positive, upbeat person.

Action Step: Smile at everyone you meet today and see what a difference it makes in your attitude.

Get Up...Get Set...Go

As a job placement counselor, I had employers tell me many times that first impressions would make the decision on whether to hire someone. One employer told me that an applicant came into his office to pick up a job application dressed in pajama pants and t-shirt. His appearance gave the impression that he was unmotivated. Your personal appearance speaks volumes about how you feel about yourself and how you want others to perceive you.

It's important to get up, get dressed, and get moving - no matter what stage in life you are in. Although I am retired, I go for a walk or to the gym in the morning and then get cleaned up and ready to start my day. It gives me a sense of accomplishment. Everyone needs to feel that emotion.

I have heard people say that they stay in their pajamas all day. They talk about being depressed and tired. I can understand that. If you don't get up and get dressed, you can't face the day. What a sad thought!

Each day we are given the gift of 24 hours to live any way that we desire. It's a gift that should not be thrown away. Life is to be lived.

Action Step: Upon awakening, s-t-r-e-t-c-h and give yourself a big hug. Take a deep breath. Savor the smell and flavor of a morning cup of coffee or tea or hot chocolate (served in a china teacup, of course). Get dressed and start moving. See how much better it feels to start your day in a relaxed manner.

An Attitude of Gratitude

You have heard this a thousand times. Be thankful. But, how many of us actually practice gratitude for everything that we have been given in our lives?

My mother always taught me to say "please" and "thank you." They are the most powerful words in your vocabulary. Counting your blessings should be done more often than just on Thanksgiving Day. It should be a daily habit. I never truly felt that deep sense of gratitude until I started writing down everything for which I was thankful each day. My list grew more each day as I started being more mindful of all of the blessings in my life - big and small.

It's easy to be thankful for the "good" in our lives. But, what about the difficult situations? Had to deal with a difficult person either at work or within your own family? Be thankful that you kept your cool. Got a speeding ticket? Be thankful that you did not have an accident. Make a game of finding something to be thankful for in every situation. Being truly grateful will make you more aware of the abundance of blessings in your life.

Action Step: Write down 5 things that you are thankful for each day. You may be pleasantly surprised at how good life has been to you!

The Technology Diet

When we go on a diet, we are told to cut down on our food intake. That's what I'm advocating here, except it's not about food. Everyone needs to cut down on our over-dependence on technology.

Yes, I am a little cynical about modern technology because I am somewhat technologically-challenged. I have, however, observed a disregard for manners and a decline in communication because of it. This isn't just about young people. It's about people of all ages.

My mother enjoyed writing notes to loved ones and taught me the value of handwritten notes. My mother died in 1991 - one week after Mother's Day - and sometimes I still read the handwritten note that she gave me on that Mother's Day. It always brings a smile to my face. My daughter just turned 40 and she wrote me a beautiful "thank you" letter for being her mother. What a gift!

And, speaking of bad manners and technology - PLEASE turn off your phone and do not text during movies, dinner, church, etc. and don't post things on Facebook or Twitter that would or could hurt others.

Action Step: Make a rule that there are no phones or computer devices being used during dinner or visits with family and/or friends. Limit yourself to checking emails, Facebook, twitter, etc. to once a day. Learn the fine art of handwritten notes - personally and professionally.

Be a Friend

I still remember a song that I sung at Camp Fire Girls Camp when I was young. The lyrics were "Make new friends, but keep the old. One is silver and the other gold." How true! My friends are the special people that I've "collected" through my lifetime - the ones from my childhood and the ones that shared common interests with me throughout the decades - through my children's activities, my career, etc. This means that our friendships will change over time as WE change.

It does not mean that we are "discarding" our friends. It just means that the friendship is taken to a new level. We put them in a special place in our hearts. It took me years to understand this. I have been truly blessed to have had so many amazing friends in 60 years. I can't help but grin when I think back over the experiences we've shared. I don't keep in touch as often as I should with friends from my past but I'm trying to get better at that. They all helped in making me the person I am today.

Always remember that a TRUE friend will see you through the good times and the bad times. They will lift you up when you are down and will encourage you to "better" yourself whether it's personal or professional.

Action Step: Call a friend today to just say "thinking of you!"

Nurture Your Relationships

If you really think about it, nurturing our relationships with others is a little overwhelming. Why? Because we have so many relationships - with our spouse, within our families, with friends, with co-workers, and even with people we encounter each day. So, how do we deal with all these people in our lives?

Being "present" when you are with them is a good start. Oftentimes we become easily distracted with everything going on in our lives. When we are talking, we are NOT listening. Listening and engaging fully in our conversations with others is the way to be in the present moment with them.

I have developed a technique that works with me whenever I am with family or friends. It's called "the three L's" - Listening, Laughing, and Loving. This technique is also a great stress reliever. If you are listening, laughing, and loving the people you are with, you will not be preoccupied with the steady stream of thoughts that enter your mind. You will be living in the "present."

Action Step: Be totally "in the moment" when you are with someone. Look into their face. Smile. Listen. If you nurture your relationships, you will be pleasantly surprised at how those relationships will flourish.

Pamper Yourself

I am amazed at how many people I know who say that they don't have time to do the things that they want to do. Even when I was working full-time and going to all of my children's activities, I still took time to do special things for myself. It kept me sane.

There is no way people can be effective in their professional or personal lives if they are frazzled. So, how do you make time for yourself? Schedule it. Make it a priority just like you make work, family, and other obligations a priority. Put it on your calendar and think of it as a "can't miss" obligation.

Discovering special ways to pamper yourself is something that you will have to figure out on your own. It can be as simple as going for a daily walk , spending 30 minutes reading a book, going for coffee at the neighborhood coffee shop, or enjoying a relaxing bubble bath.   It could even be something that requires more time or planning, such as going to a Sunday afternoon movie or scheduling a monthly massage.

Pampering yourself is not selfish. You have to love yourself first before you can spread love to others.

Action Step: Write a list of things that you like to do and which give you joy. Do one thing on that list at least once a week. You owe it to yourself. Enjoy!

Quiet Your Mind

Sometimes my mind just seems to race. Many thoughts - thoughts about the past, thoughts about the future, thoughts about my "to do" list, etc.

Those thoughts not only clutter my mind but lend themselves to a lot of unnecessary "worry" as well. I cannot believe how much time during my 60 years have been wasted with thoughts and worries that never occurred!

I have found that I am more optimistic about life when I quiet my mind. It sounds like a simple thing to do, but it is difficult at first. I would sit quietly and clear my thoughts, but then something would pop in my mind and I was back to lots of thoughts racing through again.

Over time, however, I have been able to quiet my mind by enlisting a technique that I refer to as my mind's "trash can." Whenever I have a thought that comes to me, I decide if it is worth the effort to think through or if it should be thrown away. I know that this won't work for everyone, but it works for me. Maybe you can develop your own technique.

Quieting your mind will not only give you an optimistic attitude, it will also give you a sense of peace.

Action Step: When worries overwhelm you, write down the worst-case scenario and possible solutions - and then throw it in a trash can. Over time, you will train yourself so that the "trash can" in your mind will take care of your worries.

Respect Diversity

As I've gotten older, I've noticed that
people have less tolerance for others who act,
think, or look different than they.   Maybe
that's why there are so many riots,
demonstrations, and senseless acts of
violence in our neighborhoods, communities,
countries, and world.

Respecting another person's opinion is
easier to do if you do two things - shut up and
listen. You don't have to agree with their
opinions. Just accept the fact that you will not
be able to CHANGE their opinions. We all
think that that we can convince people to see
things our way. Again, you cannot change

another person's opinion. You MIGHT be able to give them something to think about, but you won't change them.

Respect other people's opinions. They have the right to think independently - just like you do. And, wouldn't this world be boring if everyone was alike? We all look differently, dress differently, and think differently. I like that. Respecting the opinions, ideas, and look of others will make us more knowledgeable of other cultures, religions, and political affiliations. Even if we don't agree with them, we are respecting them for giving us another way to view the world.

Action Step: Listen with an empathetic ear to others. You may seriously disagree with them, but you can kindly agree to disagree without being disrespectful.

Read

One of the things I looked forward to as a child was going to the library. There was something about the quiet, the browsing of rows of books, and even the smell that was comforting to me. I know that sounds crazy to a lot of people, but I'm sure that there are many adults my age who understand that feeling. A library card is free and, therefore, it is an inexpensive way to entertain yourself or your children.

The library was a place where my imagination could soar - going to faraway lands and solving mysteries. Carefully choosing a book could take an hour or more.

After the librarian stamped the "due date" in the back of the book, I would anxiously head home to start reading.

Reading books has always provided me an escape to travel, try new adventures, laugh, and to cry. There have been books that have provided me comfort during difficult periods and books that have helped me understand things that I couldn't understand on my own.

Now that I am a grandmother, books have taken on a new meaning. I can now share books with my grandchildren. It's gratifying to see my precious grandchildren enjoying the same books that I enjoyed as a child.

Action Step: Get a library card today! Reading a good book is relaxing and fun.

Travel through Life

Ask a person what they want to do when they retire and the most common answer is "travel." But why wait until retirement? Before I retired when people would say "travel," my mind immediately went to thoughts of exotic destinations. After all, that's what I saw in the movies. But, I've come to find out that travel can be defined in many ways.

I am retired now and have done some traveling. I feel that travel is a tool for personal growth. It takes you out of your own environment and immerses you into someone else's environment. My most memorable and enjoyable trips are the ones where I soaked up the local culture, visited with fellow travelers, and kept a flexible itinerary. No rigid itineraries!

Traveling does not have to be expensive. Find a nearby city with a zoo, park, or museum and talk to the curator. Take a picnic lunch and take a walk and observe the people, sights, and sounds around you. More importantly, unplug your devices - no email, texts, Facebook, etc. Traveling can also be a great way to meet people so being able to communicate with others is important. Turn off your phones and computers. Just relax and be aware of your surroundings. Enjoy!

Action Step: Take "mental" pictures of your adventures so that they will stay in your heart and mind. You can close your eyes and re-live those trips whenever you desire.

Clear the Clutter

Want an easy way to de-stress your life? Get rid of the clutter! Clearing out the clutter from your home as well as your office or work environment will automatically clear the clutter that clouds your mind.

In order to prevent being overwhelmed at first, just start the de-cluttering process with one drawer or a table top. Throw away all old papers, magazines, junk mail, etc. If you haven't touched it in the past week, it needs to go. Put a basket nearby for bills and other important mail. Take one hour each night to go through the basket and take care of business. You can use this same process in your work environment. Take a few minutes before you leave each day to clean your desk/work station and organize it for the next day.

Go through your closets and kitchen cabinets in the same way. If you haven't worn it or used it in the past year, it needs to be sold in a garage sale or donated to charity. If you don't love it, get rid of it.

Walking into a well-organized living space and an uncluttered work environment will automatically give you a feeling of being in control which, in turn, will make you feel joyful, not stressful.

Action Step: Get started today - simplify, simplify, simplify!

Walk

How many of you have bought treadmills which, over a period of time, became a clothes rack?

I hear a lot of people say that they can't exercise because they don't have the money to join a gym or they don't have the time. Life has taught me that we all have time for the things that are important to us. Taking care of our bodies SHOULD be important to us.

Taking a walk each day takes very little time and costs nothing. It also helps to get outside and enjoy some fresh air each day. It can be for 15 minutes or an hour. It's totally up to you. Walking each day affords you the flexibility of when and where you exercise.

You don't have to drive across town to a gym

or buy new workout clothes. All you need is a

good pair of sneakers or walking shoes.

Walking not only has health benefits, but

also has a "calming" effect on our minds. By

focusing on our surroundings, we can clear

our minds of the worries and stressors of our

day. Enjoy a walk and enjoy your day!

Action Step: Include walking in your busy day by parking
far away in parking lots where you shop or work. Take
stairs instead of the elevators. Get up a little earlier each
morning and take a walk in your neighborhood before you
start your day. Start a regular "walking" routine and see
how much better you feel - physically and mentally - after
just 3 weeks.

Abandon "Old" Thinking

Am I old? No way! I am celebrating the opportunity to experience life as a 60-year-old. There are so many things that I want to do.

There are a lot of ways to "age." It's totally up to you. I have observed people who retire and they dedicate their lives to their grandchildren. I have observed people who retire and travel or move to a warmer climate. I have observed people who retire and take up new hobbies, volunteer, or start new careers. All of those things are great and keep your mind active.

It's important to keep physically active as well. Take up a sport or activity that will keep you physically fit. You also need to make sure to dress in a way that is becoming to YOU - not someone else. I cringe when I see men and women of my age dress like teenagers. It just makes them look older.

Most importantly, keep a strong support network around you. I have been truly blessed with a wonderful network of family and friends - past and present - in which to share the triumphs and tribulations of life. They all help in keeping me young. Like a fine wine, I am getting better with age!

Action Step: Write down some things that you've always wanted to learn and then try them (golf, tennis, sewing, painting, sculpture, etc.) Learning something new will keep life interesting - and keep you young at heart!

Laugh

My mom would always tell me, "laughter is the best medicine." It's certainly true. Laughter makes you feel good and gives you a positive, optimistic outlook on life.

Laughter is a great way to add joy to your life because it strengthens your relationships with others. It actually attracts others to us because people want to be around other people who find humor in bad situations and project an aura of happiness.

What is the number one way to bring more humor into your life? First of all, take yourself less seriously. Laugh at yourself (yes, those embarrassing moments are actually

humorous). Also, keep things in perspective.
Sometimes the answer to our problems lies in
seeing the humor in a situation. See the
lighter side of life by realizing that many things
in life are beyond your control - especially
other people's behavior. It is unhealthy and
unproductive to take on everyone else's
problems.

Just remember that when you laugh, you
can look at life with a more relaxed, positive,
and balanced viewpoint. Want one more
reason to laugh? You can't feel sad if you're
laughing. Enjoy a laugh today!

Action Step: Laugh out loud today when you hear a joke or
watch a funny movie or television show. See how much
better you feel after a good laugh.

Worry is Unnecessary

"If we spend our time with regrets over yesterday, and worries over what might happen tomorrow, we have no today in which to live."

Author Unknown

Worry is the fear of the unknown. It is the thought that the worst will happen and it is basically useless and serves no purpose. It can affect us physically, causing us to lose sleep and/or overindulging in food or alcohol.

Consider the following statistics:

40% of what we worry about never happens;
30% has already happened, so accept it for what it is;
12% is needless worry, such as what other people think of us;

10% is not important, such as what we are going to wear or fix for dinner;
4% actually happens but is beyond our control (natural disasters, etc.)
4% is the result of our actions and is part of who we are.

In order to alleviate worry, ask yourself 2 questions:

1) What is the worst that can possibly happen? Get mentally prepared to accept the worst possible scenario. Then, try to improve upon the worst.

2) Will this matter a year from now? More often than not, the situation is not as important as you have made it out to be. If it won't matter a year from now, the source of worry is just an irrelevant detail in your life.

Action Step: Worrying is wasted time. Use the same energy for doing something about whatever worries you.

No Regrets

The definition of regret is "to feel sorry, disappointed, or distressed about." All of us have regrets - things we wish we had done differently, paths we should or should not have taken in our lives. Regrets result from questioning the course our lives have taken as a result of the decisions we have made.

The problem with having regrets is that they are mentally taxing. It is a way of refusing to let go of something and they become part of us. As a result, it becomes difficult to enjoy and appreciate the good things in your present life.

There are, however, ways to re-frame our regrets. Think of regrets as learning opportunities.   When you find yourself thinking of the regret, turn your thoughts to the things you have learned and the opportunities that are now yours - even if they have not been what you would have preferred. Look for the lesson and focus on it. Accept "what is" instead of what could have been.

More importantly, NEVER regret anything that makes you smile. Forget regrets or life is yours to miss.

Action Step: Watch the movie "It's a Wonderful Life." It's a Christmas movie, but can be watched at any time of year. It has a good message about living life with no regrets. You define your own life.

Accept Change

As someone who likes to be in control, accepting changes is very hard for me. I like routine and familiarity. Life, however, is unpredictable and so changes are inevitable.

A "tradition" is something that remains the same over time. But, does it really? My mother hosted Christmas dinner for her brothers and their families for over 20 years. Over time, however, it was impossible to get everyone together for our big "cousin" Christmas. My aunts and uncles eventually started hosting Christmas for their own children and grandchildren. My mother changed our traditional gathering into something that worked for us and our changing lives as we grew up and moved away. Some years we celebrated on Christmas Day and some years we celebrated Christmas on another day, but it was always wonderful no matter when we celebrated. Traditions change as do families.

Life is all about change. A spouse dies suddenly, children grow up and start their own families, and people retire from life-long careers. These events all lead to changes and choices to be made. A new chapter in your life begins!

Action Step: Embrace change. View it as an opportunity for personal growth. If you face a change in your life and make a choice that goes against what everyone else thinks, the world will not fall apart. Accepting change can be liberating!

Face Reality

Reality programs have taken over television programming and I am afraid that it has distorted our vision of reality.

The first step to facing reality is to realize that you are the sum of your life experiences - some good and some not so good. You are who you are. You cannot compare yourself to others because you are unique. What you see on television is not your reality. So, don't live in "TV land" or "some day" world ("some day" when I lose weight or get married or find the perfect job, etc.). Those thoughts will only frustrate you.

Instead, be proud of that person looking back at you in the mirror - all the imperfections included. That is what makes you unique and special.

Try to be grateful for each moment of your life - including those moments in which you struggle. It will really make a difference in your life if you look at each moment of your life as a gift. You would not ignore a gift, so do not ignore the time you have been given. Don't dwell on the past or worry about the future. So, start start facing your reality NOW. You are unique and special - imperfections and all.

Action Step: Be true to yourself. Accept your present circumstances in life. Look in the mirror and smile at that person. That's the real, wonderful YOU!!

The Secret to Having It All

I saved this for last because it is the most important. I thought about this long and hard. I'm 60 years old and have have spent most of my life striving to have it all. So, what is this big secret to being successful?

The secret to having it all is to realize you already do.

That sounds simple enough, but it is very hard for most people to grasp. We are so caught up in "keeping up with the Jones's" that we forget about all that we already have.

We live in a world of instant gratification. If we want something, we go out and buy it on credit. If we are sad, we are told to "snap out of it." We all tend tend to think about a perfect life for ourselves instead of facing the fact that no life is perfect. We all face struggles, disappointments, and frustrations - even the "Jones's." And, yes, it is perfectly normal to have sadness from time to time. It's okay. Just don't let yourself be sad because you are comparing yourself to others. Get over the "poor me" thinking. You have power and control over your emotions. Enjoy - and really experience - every moment that you have on this earth.

Action Step: Be kind. Be compassionate. Count your blessings - big and small. Remember that you make this world a better place by enriching the lives of others. Most importantly, remember that you are loved!

A Final Thought...

You are a wonderful person. Don't look back. Take a deep breath and go forward. Too many people wait for change to come into their lives to move forward. Don't wait. Be the person you have always wanted to be - NOW!

Get a vision in your mind of what you want your life to resemble - and then "live" that vision. Strife and trauma may come your way, but those things can set you up for the best things that ever happened to you. You have wisdom and strength. Ignore questions and gossip as you make your path toward being the person you want to be. Give yourself a chance. You deserve it!

"The people who get on in this world are the people who get up and look for the circumstances they want, and, if they can't find them, make them." - George Bernard Shaw

About the Author

Janet Burke currently lives in Edmond, Oklahoma and is retired after a career as a social worker and counselor. She was the Coordinator of the Single Parent/Displaced Homemaker Program at a Career & Technology Center in Oklahoma and served as the State Director of SkillsUSA Oklahoma (a Career Tech student organization for students enrolled in Trade & Industrial programs).

She was honored as the Outstanding Member of the National Career & Technology Education Equity Council in 2004 and inducted into the Technology Students Association Hall of Fame in 2011. She was appointed by the Governor of Oklahoma to the State Employee Assistance Program Advisory Council in 2012.

She truly believes and lives by the motto: "Attitude is Everything."